# PRAISE!

## POEMS

Mary Harwell Sayler

CLADACH
Publishing

PRAISE! Poems
© 2017 by Mary Harwell Sayler

An AGATES Book of Poetry

Published by
Cladach Publishing
PO Box 336144
Greeley, CO 80633
http://cladach.com

Cover Art: © Can Stock Photo / Vapi
Interior Art: © Can Stock Photo / longquattro

ISBN-13: 9781945099038
ISBN-10: 194509903
Library of Congress Control Number: 2017934807

Printed in the U.S.A.

*To Bob*


*Praise God our Father!*
*Blessings on our Mother Earth.*
*We are their love child.*

# CONTENTS

# A WORD FROM THE POET

Some time ago, I asked, "Is there something You want me to do, Lord?" and, immediately, the word "Praise" came to mind. Having been raised in a polite Christian family, the inclination to thank God and people came easily enough, but praise? Frankly, I wasn't sure I knew what praising God truly meant—or at least how it differed from thanksgiving.

After looking up several dictionary definitions, I saw praise as expressing approval more than the appreciation shown in giving thanks. Praise commends, lauds, and says good things—not with gratitude in mind so much as acknowledgement, commendation, and re-commendation. Or, to say it another way, praise focuses on Who God Is, more than what God does. Praise pours out our love to the Lord.

The Psalms provide wonderful examples of ways to praise, pray, thank God—and lament. A closer than usual study of those priceless poems shows that almost all of the lamentations begin with a concern or complaint but end with purposeful thanks or praise. That uplift at the end exemplifies a strong faith in God, despite the circumstances, and also shows how a poured-out heart must remain completely honest and wholly vulnerable.

Ready to praise but not particularly practiced, I immediately sensed God's help as relevant thoughts and phrases caught my attention each morning. Once I had typed those beginning lines in a computer file, other thoughts and lines swiftly followed—somewhat like a stream-of-consciousness flow, but more "subconscious" or even "unconscious" of what might come next.

Although praise-poems began to come to me regularly, their titles did not! Normally, I'm an advocate of titling poems and have always done so in writing free verse and traditional forms, but this time seemed different. This time felt more like writing "contemporary psalms." Instead of titling them with sequential numbers, as did Bible editors in identifying biblical Psalms, the first line of each poem became its title and an integral part of its reading.

Spontaneity also remained key—often with a phrase that startled me or an insight God gave in thoughts I'd never had before the poem gained my attention. So my "method" became an intent to obey, rather than create, as I wrote down each spontaneous thought or phrase with the anticipation that the rest of the words would freely follow. Most of the time they did, sometimes even exploding onto the page. Other times they seemed more reflective, depending, perhaps, on my mood or something God wanted me to consider as I wrote to discover what the lines had to say.

When each contemporary psalm seemed to have finished speaking, I posted it on the Praise Poems blog I'd created just for this, with no thoughts of a book until—after about a year—the poems suddenly ceased to flow. Even then, I felt too disappointed to think beyond my feelings. So it took a while before it occurred to me, "This might be a book." I then welcomed the idea with the title of *PRAISE!* in big caps and fireworks exploding on the front cover to show how the writing had felt, but, more, to show readers—to show you—that praise poems and contemporary psalms also await you as you pray, listen, and begin to write down what comes to you.

Maybe you'll prefer to call such poems "meditations." Maybe you'll see them as prayers. Maybe you'll glimpse something poetic and realize you like poetry reading and writing more than you ever thought! Or maybe you'll be stunned by the raw thoughts and ragged edges that need to be heard.

Thanks to the thoughtful suggestions of my editor-publisher, poet Catherine Lawton, the edges in these poems have been smoothed considerably! In previous poetry-writing adventures, I've been inclined to let poems flow, then I let them sit awhile before reading them aloud and revising anything in need of clarification or amplification. This time, though, I merely noted and collected the praise poems with little "tweaking" for poetic effect until receiving and responding to Cathy's helpful comments.

As you read through the results, I pray these contemporary psalms will speak to and for you so much that you'll want to return to them again. More important, I pray this book encourages you to talk with God—openly, honestly, and regularly.

May the Lord bless you and your life of purposeful praise.

Mary Harwell Sayler
Lake Como, Florida

Rejoicing in God's Attributes and Character—with

# Praise

## Praise Our God Who Prays For Us—

Prays for us to listen
and walk in the Way of the Lord.

Then, God's Hand will restrain
every hand lifted against us.

Then, the Hand of the Lord will protect us
and feed us honey from the Rock.

## Praise God Our Axis—

Around Whom
all things turn
and without Whom
everything gets
off balance—
like an overloaded
washing machine
or like earth off its orbit
or a planet spinning
out of control.

Praise God our pivot point
around Whom our whole lives revolve.

## Clothed In Light, My Lord I Praise—

Your pure patina that plays
   throughout the universe—
   the radical radiance
   of Your love for us,
   the shine of truth
You bring in Your Word,
   the gift of Your glow
   set in a bright ring around us—
   as we ask for Your insight
   and bask in Your light.

## Praise Our Playful God—

Who created us
   from dirt
   and earth-mud—

Like a Holy Child
   molding
   modeling clay,

Loving the results,
   but wanting more:

Wanting joy
   to mobilize us,

Wanting love
   to propel us,

Wanting us
   to respond to Him.

## Praise God the Breath of Life—

Who breathed me awake
  at birth,

Who breathes on me now
  in my sleep,

Who keeps my lungs filled
  with Holy Spirit *Ruah*,
  and takes my breath away.

## Holy Heart of My Heart—

I praise you for purging
these surges of self
that get in Your way
when I want mine.

Praise You, Lord God,
for Your pure heart
and holy veins flowing
with the kind of kindness
I want to be
the finer part of me.

Praise You for oozing out
whatever I complain about,
and please empower me
to trust You hour by hour
and day by day, as I pray
for what I can't begin to do
without a heart transplant
from You.

## Oh My Darling Jesus—

I love You, love You, Lord.
I love how You look deep into my eyes
and see something of Yourself.

I love how You quiet my storms
and rebuke ill will around me.

When I'm feverish with activity
or sink over my head in hot water,
I love how You take my hand
  and lift me up
  to breathe.

Each time I die inside
You call me
forth by name
and bring me
into Your living Light.

**Praise You, Jesus, For Showing Us God—**

Whom
I could no more picture than
helium in a balloon
until You gave fresh vision
of God-flesh,
bones, blood,
and body cells
drawn as circular wells,
filled
with love and life
and living water.

### Praise God Who Listens—

When no one else will,
when no one else notices
our problem,
our pain,
or the terrible loneliness
that comes in dark hours,
when only our
"God Who listens"
truly hears and responds.

## Praise God the Present—

Tense of the verb "to be"—
The One Who Is
always here,
the great I Am
in Whom
you are,
we are,
they are,
I Am.

Praise God
the Ever-Present One.

### Praise God Our Praise—

Without Whom
there is none:
   no cause for joy,
   no source of love,
   no hope of peace.

Praise God Who dwells
in us and around us—
enthroned on our praises—
uplifting our days.

## Praise God Who Sees—

The big picture, the cosmic view—
like we do when we look
    at that ant-hill-in-the-making,
    while waiting for the school bus.

How like us, those ants!
Watching them, we wondered why
    they picked that particular spot
    for a home when other areas
    would be better by far.

But that's how ants are:
they only see what they can see
in front of them on a lowly level—
    like we do when we're blocked
    by our own low view that few
    ever go beyond.

Praise our Most-High God Who sees
precisely where and what we need to be.

## Praise God the Good—

Without Whom we'd have no
  goodness.

Praise God the Good
  for the good we discern
  in ourselves and all
  creation.

Praise our Good God
  for making us in
  the very image of Good.

Imagine that!

Oh, imagine that image
  of God-goodness
  in you, in them, in me.
  Look for it! Look for it!
See.

## Praise Christ Our Lover—

Who woos us with lilies,
serenades us with sparrows,
feeds us good grain
and fine wine
poured
from His vintage collection—
our very selves blended—
made one by His love.

## Praise God Our Holy Parent—

Our Father-Mother-Holy-Love,
Who's wholly perfect, wholly
  present, wholly ours.

Praise God our Heavenly Mommy,
  Mama, Mom, Mum, Ma,

Who never ever breaks
  a dish,
  a bone,
  a word of promise.

Praise God our Heavenly Papa,
Poppy, Daddy, Dad,
Who never breaks—
  Who never ever breaks.

## Praise God For Stillness—

For the quietness within
with which I hear You speak—
not audibly so much as
inner knowing,
a silent word reassuring me
of Your presence,
guiding, comforting,
quieting my soul to hear,
to heed, to follow
Your leading in my life—
unending inhalation
of Your inaudible breath.

## Praise God the Rock—

Under Whom I crawl
when I feel low,
the Rock I climb
to get a higher view.

Praise God, the Rock
Who rolled aside
as Jesus died,
then rolled away
as Christ arose—
from the unclosed tomb.

## Praise God For Being Faithful—

For filling us with faith—
real faith that believes
God means what He says.

Our kin in the Garden
didn't have that kind of faith,
but Noah did
in desert-like drought
when God said, "Build a boat."

And Abraham had faith
to believe God had reasons
for saying, "Go!"

And Moses had faith
God meant each word
said to Pharaoh.

Praise God for giving us
faith to know
God means what He says
when, through Christ,
He forgives us;
when, through Christ,
He gives us
His power, His authority;
when, in the church,
He calls us Christ's body.

## Praise God Our Heavenly Fog—

Through Whom we see what's now
and near and clear enough to touch.

Praise God Who shows us all we
need to know and just how much.

Praise our heavenly mist, Who holds
the mystery of the sacred, the divine,
and lifts us to Himself in bread, in wine.

## Praise the Love Who Never Leaves Us—

No matter how little
we think of ourselves
or even how little
we give thought to God.

Praise God Who is Love,
Who was Love, Who will
be Love,
Who fills
us with an infinite store of
loving care that lifts us
from the bottom of a barrel
and sends us on the Way.

**Praise God Our Taxi Driver—**

With Whom we fare well
yet pay only interest.

Praise Christ our divine driver,
Who knows the best route
and takes us
where we're meant to go,
then stays with us
when we think we have arrived.

Praise our most holy chauffeur,
Who gets us safely through
danger and dark places en route
to our heavenly destination.

## Praise Jesus the Way—

Without Whom we would be lost—
like Dante in the dark forest
or Hansel and Gretel in the woods
with a witch waiting to devour.

Praise Jesus our way on earth
to be forgiven and live our lives
in the kingdom of Heaven—
God's kingdom ruled by Love.

Praise Jesus the only way
of safe passage into the sphere
of the spirit world where
nothing holy harms—and where,
Praise Christ, we'll have infinite
access to the comfort of His arms.

## Praise God Who Speaks—

To us through nature, other
people, communion, and,
most expressly, through
God's Word—

Made manifest in Christ Jesus,
made readable in holy Scriptures,
made one in us as we read
and heed the Lord through our
own words, deeds, and actions.

But how can we obey if we've
never *read God?*

How can we know what to do
if we've never received the Word
of Christ, Who comes to us—

Living, dying, rising, and writing
Himself into our lives in Holy
Spirit power and earth-braille?

## Lord, Your Love Extends—

To a thousand generations of mine;
for each time one person believes
in You and receives Your salvation, the next
thousand generations continue on in You too!

When I think of how You left the ninety-nine
to look for a single lamb who was lost, I find
myself less worried about my kids. They're
Your children too, Lord! Praise God! Praise
God, and thank goodness! The goodness
of our loving God goes on throughout eternity—
in your family and mine—in you, in them, in me.

## Praise Christ Our Holy Telescope—

Through Whom we clearly see
  what's coming
  when we need to know.

Praise Christ our holy
microscope
Who helps us to discern
  the true,
  the false
  in tiny telling details.

Praise You, Christ,
our perfect lens
through Whom we view
  ourselves, our lives, our
  church, our world, and You.

## Praise You God Our Tutor—

For instructing us in the love life
You want us to live,

For training us through
Christ Jesus and Your Word,

For coaching us with the help
of Holy Spirit and the counsel
of good friends who have
suffered through the ache
of daily living and have
come to know You well—
who have consistently come to ask,
"Lord, what's the loving thing to do?"

## Praise God the Creator—

Of all good!

Praise God the Father
of all pure love.

Praise God the sower,
Who seeds our soiled selves
with Holy Spirit,

Nurturing praise and all
blessed notions that
spring to our minds
like flowers.

## Praise God Your Lover—

Who embraces you
like a blanket wrapped
around the chill of your life
and holds you—
   insulated from evil,
   protected from attack,
   cloistered in comfort,
   cocooned in Christ—

Until, reassured,
you risk life again
and rise in the lift of God's love.

## Praise Christ Our Body—

Who holds us together
in cell and membrane,
tissue and blood,
tendon and tears.

Praise Christ Whose body
embraces
each part of us—
an ear, an eye, a knee,
a scalp, a head of hair
with each curl counted.

Praise Christ Who gave
His body and
welcomes each one of us—

Into the body of Christ,
the Church—

To work, to play
and pray together,
to love and forgive,
to worship as One Being
the Lord we adore.

## Praise God Our Praise—

Without Whom
  nothing
    we have done or will do
    will be worth mentioning.

Praise God our praise
  to Whom we raise
    our hands in worship,
  for Whom we stretch
    our fullest selves—
reaching toward the Lord.

Petitions, Thanksgivings, Confessions
and Longings Expressed through

# Prayer

## Here I Am, Lord, Ready—

Ready to listen,
ready to pray,
ready to watch You
and be amazed,
ready to thank You
and give You praise.

## O You Who Test the Mind—

And heart,
let no enemy find my soul
apart from You—
  my One True Cause
  for consistent praise.

Let me know
if I persist on paths
  apart from You.
Assess me, Lord,
  insistently.

## Help Us, Lord, To Find the Way Back—

To what You want for us.
How easy it is to get off track
without meaning to or realizing
what we've done is wrong!

Forgive us for thinking ill
of Your anointed
when a pastor, parent,
peoples, or church
need healing prayers.

Help us to praise You, Lord—
Father of all and worthy of all
praise—no matter what
situations raise themselves
against us.

May we come to full attention,
live loyally in Your intention,
and forgive,
forgive, forgive.

## Jesus Asks, *Why?*

*Why did you doubt Me?*
*Why did you have little faith?*
*Don't you know I Am?*

Oh, Lord, heal my unbelief!

Help me to raise my eyes toward You.
Help me to find relief in praise.

## Lord, Help Me To Bear—

Your Good News when I feel
as though I have none.

Help me to bear Your love
when I've descended low.

Help me to bear this lift
of praise for Your compassion.

# What Do I Do, Lord—

When I'm feeling overwhelmed
by waves of work or worry—
   without a moment to breathe
   deeply enough to perceive
   my need to pray?

I don't want to keep sighing
   or fixing my focus on
   anything but You!

And yet, I do.

Forgive me, Father! Lift
me higher than this heaviness
   and into a deep desire
   of heavenly praise to You.

## Thumbs Don't Seem Important, Lord—

Until we lose one
or a stiff joint begins to bend
like a rusted hinge.

How brilliantly
You have made us, and yet
we cringe at the sight
of our roller-coaster-looking skin.

Can any sin compare to our lack
of praise?

Forgive us, Lord, for thinking thumbs
are not important
or forgetting how much we need them
to open an obstinate jar or push
in a thumb tack or click our fingers in time
to music.

Praise You, Lord, for placing
flexible thumbs on hands
intended to serve You.

Help us to give
a thumbs-up to every part
of the brilliantly beautiful
body of Christ.

## How Can I Praise You, Lord—

When grief and grievances
fill my head?—

Forgive me, God,
for complaints negating all
I have to be grateful for; not
only Your good gifts, but Your
wholly reliable guidance that
my grumblings show I do not
trust as much as I once thought.

## In the Wake of So Much Hate and Killing—

Help us, Lord, to be willing to praise You
for Jesus' sake. Fill us with Your mercy
and unadulterated care to pass
along to peoples everywhere as we
pray for You to "Forgive them, Father,
for they know not what they do." And,
Lord Jesus, as You shed Your blood
for us, we thank You for the flood
of people giving their blood today,
so the injured may keep on living—
healed by Your love—and forgiving.

## Praying the Lord's Prayer for the Nations

Our Father Who is in Heaven,
blessed and sacred is Your Name.

May Your kingdom come
to our country and all continents—
to reign over us with justice, mercy,
and love, and may Your will prevail
on earth as it does in Heaven.

Lord, give us this day's sustenance
for our mental, physical, and spiritual
well-being, but also our
social and emotional health.

Forgive us for getting out of bounds
and forgetting to forgive each person
—past or present—who has ever
intruded against us.

Lead us not into temptation
to do wrong or cause harm
or give in to fears and disbelief;
but deliver us from evil,
apathy, and cruelties of all kinds.

For Yours is the kingdom we want!
Yours is the power we need.
Yours is the glory we worship
and adore in the Name
of Christ Jesus our Lord.
Amen.

## Father, I Wish You Would Come Home—

And throw down Your keys
and take off Your watch
and empty Your pockets
of change like my dad did
every night of my child life.

But, oh. Is that what *You*
want from *me*?

Help me, Heavenly Father,
to come home to You and
always keep watch but
put down my keys and

Change.

# How Far Above Politics You Are, O Lord—

High above the low-slung mud
and lack of love shown for others,
   including our own country.

Let us be a nation who dwells in You.

Let Your justice reign!
Let Your regard for every person
   be the law
   by which we guard ourselves from error.

Bind the terror and troubles
   that tear us apart
   or make us tremble and fade
   into our fears.

Raise us above the dust
from which we are made—
   the earth shade in which we hide.

Give us ways to praise You,
O God Most High.
Lift our lonely lives—
and politics—to the sky!

Celebrating and Meditating on Jesus' Sacrifice, Death, and
Resurrection into Eternal Life.

# Easter

## May I Wash Your Feet, Lord?

I'd be happy to rinse away
the earth dirt and scrub
Your sandals—much happier
than if You asked to clean my feet.

On Maundy Thursday, some of us
go up for a foot-washing at church,
and I am embarrassed when a man
with feet two-thirds the size of mine
takes my foot in his hands and begins
to wash without a word.

Oh.
Yes, Lord.
I'd be happier
if You held the foot I
once withheld from You.

Thank You
for grooming us to be Your
less conceited servants.

## Praise God Our Heavenly Father—

Who wooed us forth from Mother Earth
and weeps and weeps for Cain, for Abel.

Praise God the Father
of our Lord Jesus, sent to save us
from ourselves: the Christ, Divine
Brother, Savior, the One Sacrifice,
Just Mediator, and Perfect Friend—able
to tend and mend our wounded Family
over whom God weeps and weeps.

## The Day Holds Its People—

To star words and crystal
globes, to apron strings
and past experiences,
to present predicaments
and verdicts of guilt.

Who so bound
can stand?

Oh, praise! Oh,
praise the Son
of Man!

Praise Christ
Who, bound
to the cross
for our sins,
willingly died.

Praise our Lord
Who cuts us free
with the sword
thrust into His side.

## Praise Christ Our Lamb—

Whose flawless skin covers
our imperfections
and wraps up God's Word,
which He fulfilled.

Praise Christ our Lamb—

Whose Body feeds us,

Whose veins
cleanse us
from vanity,

Whose love weaves us
warmly into His wool.

## My God! My God, Why Have You Forsaken—

Your life for mine?

Why are You so far from helping
Your own holiness
by taking on my sins?

You magnetized crowds
with Your love
and prayers and healing touch,
only to draw sin from me—
like a magnet cast in iron
nails that tear away
Your hands.

Why would You suffer such torment
except for pure love only You can know?

My God! My God,
please accept my wholly
inadequate repentance
and praise.

## My Jesus, I Love You—

For loving me.
I praise You
for living free of sin,
despite more temptations
than most men must endure.

On the cross You could
have turned the wood
back into the tree
knowing good and evil,
but You chose to be
the Final Offering,
the Last Sacrifice,
the Tree of Life turned
toward me in love.

## Beside My Desk, Seashells—

Show evidence of life
outgrowing the old self
and discarding hard
   protective layers
   that once encompassed
   vulnerabilities.

Praise You, Lord! You
have risen from the grave
condition of mankind
and found Yourself
   buoyed in the Spirit
   but anchored in us,
Your blessed Body on earth.

### Praise Christ Our Purifier—

Who filters the spite from our souls
and decontaminates our spirits;

Who cleanses us from all dross
and removes anything ill or gross
from our memories and old ways
of doing things. Christ we praise—

For bathing us with His blood
on His cross of wood, cleansing us
from sin, and forgiving us for good.

## Praise God For Sabbath Rest—

That space between work weeks
which our Creator first enjoyed
as the Father making time
to take pleasure in the very
good children He created.

Praise God the Son
for the rest from death
that came to us on Easter—
the first Resurrection Day
and rebirth of boundless life.

Praise God the Holy Spirit
for the rest of Pentecost
lived out each day—
first as we cease striving
for that perfection
we'll never obtain
on our own—and then
for trusting God
to hold us, to love us,
forgive us and uplift
the rest of our lives.

## Hallelujah! Hallelujah!

Christ our Lord
is risen
in each of us each day,
and neither gravity
nor a cruel grave
can keep us down.

Responding to GOD through the Lens of

# Creation

## The Heavens Belong To You, O Lord

You've given the earth
   to the children of mankind,
   but we are not kind.

We've tarred the land
   with roads and killed
   what scared us and tilled
   under trees and drained
   swamps and fueled the
   ozone with jet streams.

We've lied to people
   we like and shown hate
   to those unlike us!

Please help us, Lord, to be
   kind to everything on earth
   and be the kind of children who
   belong with You in Heaven.

## What's Wrong With Us?

Can't we stop rejecting
   the bats feeding on bugs,
   the snakes reducing rats,
   the politicians in need
   of prayer and protection.

Praise the Lord! Praise
You, Lord!

Nothing—
   nothing is wrong with You!

## Consider the Dandelions, How They Grow—

Dense and golden in some places
   with bright yellow faces almost every-
   where, but sparse and delicate here.

It's weird how they're looked on as weeds
   when we can eat each part but seeds—
   even steeping tea from the roots or cooking
   the young tender shoots of leaves as greens.

I've seen how children love to blow the
   seeded pinwheels, white as snow, to fill
   the air with possibilities of dandy wine
   and dandy tea and little lion heads and
   handy food and wildflowers—so good
   to consider as we raise our heads and
   hands and hearts—and all of our most
   useful parts—in thanks to God, and praise.

## Zebra Stripes Abbreviated—

In a butterfly wing…

The mango head of a condor
—orange-pink
as Pacific sunsets…

The spokes of an umbrella
folding and unfolding the arms
of a bat in a cavern,
dark, damp, and deep.

What wonder! What beauty!
What wit You have written
into creation, O Creator God.

## Praise Our God For the Grandeur—

Known in the apricot sky,
    casting a velvety glow over
    the pond and lily pads
    before bursting into orange
    flames behind the black-
    barked forest to the west.

Praise God for the grandeur
    shown in mountain peaks,
    the ocean's wild waves,
    stars drawing incandescent
    pictures in the sky, and a
    newborn child's first cry.

## The Owl Did Not Call My Name But—

Flew by without a sound—
barely above the ground—before
   landing on a lower branch
   of the cedar we call "Leb"

Then turning its back to me
to display grey-brown feathers
   dappled in white to match
   the tree's catch of sun.

The owl still did not call
nor ask the important question:
   *Who? Who?*
But I know, Lord, it's You—
the One Who truly knows
   my name.

## Into the World With Wonder—

Spring comes quietly at first, before
azaleas burst, showering us with pink
petals freckled at the center, followed by
magnolia blossoms showing pear-
shaped petals—creamy-white and
cupped to catch the sun. Tails flagging,
squirrels hop across the meadow and
run along the arms of oak, playing tag.

Catch me, Lord. Tag me as Your own.
Let me spring into Your arms, ready to
soak up the Son with my arms raised
in praise of You and worlds of wonder.

## Praise God For the Spider Plant—

The elegant drape of its variegated leaves,
   tipped in tiny white flowers
   and tasseled with new growth.

Praise God for my father,
   whose hands, still shaky from a stroke,
   sifted soil to pot the first of these plants
   now nestled in my yard for many years.

Praise God for new growth
   continuing to spring forth—
   reminding me of constant love
   and ongoing life in You.

## My World Has Grown Too Small, Lord—

Housebound by kids and work and weather,
I've longed for outdoor days, and now they come!

Embryonic leaves unfurl their yellow-green,
and winds cause applause among the oaks.
Pink azalea blossoms blink long lashes,
and bird and squirrels set to building nests.

The sky pitches pillowy clouds against
a bright blue blanket, stretching to infinity;
and my world expands behind the universe
to catch a glimpse of all in praise of You.

## Even If the Hawk Kills—

Colorful songbirds in our yard,
I praise You for the birds of prey,
    who lift us as they soar
    majestically.

And even if the coral snake
hides poison beneath our shed,
I praise You for designing such
    flamboyant
    bands of beauty.

And though the bougainvillea stabs
with its long thorns, I praise You
for reminders of Your crown
    and the beautiful red flowers
    bleeding on the lawn.

## Still Standing

The wind snaps its fingers;
our oak tree drops on command;
palm fronds lay prostrate. Rain
washes—band after band
of purifying power
from the Lord's cleansing hand.
Faith and spider webs still stand.

## The Universe Sings of the Glory of God—

And the Word can be heard to the ends
of the world!

Listen! Hear the happy hum of
   bees, the melodic call of a wren,
   the swoosh of eagle's wings,
   the cattle in a far-off field.

Can you hear the trees clapping
   for *Ruah,* or the ocean's surf
   slapping the shore with waves
   of applause?

May we and all creation find the key
to sing praise to God in harmony!

Praise in Moments of Surprise, Awe and

# Wonder

### Christ In Me and I In Him—

What a glorious hope and calling!

The Lord seeks me and sometimes finds
    a preoccupied mess
    caught up in my own
    busy-ness.

What kind of sanctuary am I?

What hope does the Lord have for me
    to empty self
    of worldly ways
    and invite Christ in—
with prayer and praise?

## In Wondrous Ways Our Lord God Works—

As we wait
tables each Thursday morning
when volunteers serve breakfast
to one-hundred people or more
who gather in our community.

By nine the rush hours end, but then
a young couple comes in late
and only asks for toast.
I bring it on a small plate
and can't help but notice
the woman seems distraught.
Her shoulders quake
as though she's seen a ghost,
but likely she has taken
a deep chill or bears some sorrow
that shakes her very core.

*What more can we serve her but prayer?*

We ask, and she says yes—
and praise God—
we find You, Lord,
in our very core, waiting tables.

## I Recognize You, Lord—

When we walk together,
 discussing scripture
 as though we're on
 the Emmaus Road.

I recognize You
 in the breaking of
 communal bread
 at Eucharist,
 family suppers
 and potluck dinners
 when we talk of You
 around the table.

Your peace I recognize
 within—and without,
 as trouble stirs
 when I forget to pray.

I recognize You, Lord,
 in inspired songs and music,
 in babies with arms upraised,
 in glowing faces, and in
worship overflowing with praise.

## God Fell In Love With Me—

And you and them, and we
did nothing to deserve this!

Sin crawled through our skin
and made us uninviting,
but God looked through
our blemishes and took
away each mark against us.

What a relief to be loved!

What a joy to be clean!

What a wonder to believe
in God's love so much, we're
happy with ourselves!

Adoring and Celebrating the CHILD of

# Christmas

## Adore, Adore Our Coming Lord—

The greatness
of Almighty God
arriving
in a newborn Child—
a baby boy
named Jesus,
Who cries for us
to hold Him close
then cradles *us*—
the infants.

## When God Gave Us Jesus—

The One Who would save us—
Heaven could not contain itself.

Light spilled from a star,
heralding His arrival.

The earth burst into life.
Birds called for revival.

And frightened shepherds
trembled like sheep

When angels awakened
their sleep with song
as light as snowflakes,
as powerful as a
tsunami of harmony
pouring onto earth
at Jesus' birth.

Oh, praise Him!

## Our Souls Proclaim the Greatness of the Lord!

Our spirits rejoice in Christ our Savior!
For the Lord has looked on us—His lowly servants—
    and given us the Baby Jesus and called us blessed.

Great things has our Almighty Father done for us
    —holy is His Name.

We who honor Him will have mercy;
  the strength of His arm will lift us up
    and fill us with His Spirit until our very souls
    levitate into the greatness of the Lord.

## Oh Come! Let Us Celebrate—

The birth of the Christ-Child
Who rejoices at our rebirth.

The Holy Infant Jesus—
dependent
on us for His care—
shows us
how we must
come to Him
like trusting children.

Hold Him on your lap
with love,
and let Him hug you,
heal you,
and hum a lullaby.

# About the Poet

Mary Harwell Sayler began reading the Bible and writing poems as a child and has never stopped. Eventually, she placed twenty-nine books in all genres with Christian and educational publishers and began leading Bible study discussions in mainline church denominations.

Over two-thousand of Mary's poems, articles, and children's stories have appeared in magazines, church take-home papers, anthologies, and e-zines. She has also written three Kindle e-books on various aspects of writing. She blogs on Bible topics and poetry.

Her published poetry books include:

*Living in the Nature Poem* (Hiraeth Press, 2012).

*Outside Eden*, a book of Bible-based poems (Kelsey Books, 2014).

*Beach Songs & Wood Chimes*, a book of children's poems (Kelsey Books, 2014).

*Faces in a Crowd* (self-published, 2016), available on Amazon and elsewhere.

The poems in this book originally appeared on her blog, *Praise Poems*. For more information visit Mary's website: http://www.marysayler.com/

CPSIA information can be obtained
at www.ICGtesting.com
Printed in the USA
LVOW11s1920281117
557885LV00006B/757/P